eggs

recipes   Jodi Liano

photographs   Kate Sears

weldon**owen**

contents

why eat eggs?

One of the most healthful foods, eggs are perfectly proportioned protein powerhouses encased in a handy little package. They are also incredibly versatile, whether used in sweet or savory dishes, eaten on their own or used as the building block for countless fabulous dishes.

From creamy mounds of scrambled eggs and fluffy omelets stuffed with cheese to delicate quiche with flaky crusts and hearty vegetable-studded frittatas, eggs are one of the most multipurpose ingredients you can find. Whether fried, poached, scrambled, baked, or boiled, used whole or separated, they are talented kitchen performers. They can be eaten by themselves or added to dishes from around the world to provide flavor, color, and consistency.

Eggs are the quintessential breakfast and brunch ingredient, but they are also suitable for a light lunch when paired with a fresh salad, or even as part of a hearty supper. The simple yet inspiring dishes found in this book include both classic comforts such as Quiche Lorraine, Toad in the Hole, and Deviled Eggs, as well as creative new ideas such as Eggs Baked in Tomatoes, Curried Eggs, and Egg, Bacon, and Brie Panini, that are sure to become part of your standard repertoire.

On their own, eggs supply a weath of vitamins, minerals, protein, and fat. In fact, egg whites are among the most healthful of foods, being both low in fat and high in protein. And while egg yolks contain most of the fat and cholesterol found in an egg, they also provide the most flavor.

a note about salt

All of the recipes in this book were prepared using kosher salt, which has a coarser grain than standard iodized salt, making it easy to grasp with your fingertips. Its light salty taste means you might use slightly more than standard salt, so always season to taste, especially when finishing a dish. Sea salt is also an excellent option, with its delicate white crystals and fine mineral taste.

There are five basic parts to every egg: shell, membrane, chalazae, yolk, and white. The oval-shaped shell is one of the strongest shapes found in nature. The inner and outer membranes protect the egg from bacteria and help keep the egg moist. The yolk contains some protein, most of the vitamins and minerals, and all of the fat. The white protects the yolk and contains most of the protein, which is one reason it is so good for us and why it whips up so well. The cloudy strings are called the chalazae, which hold the yolk in the center of the egg white.

buying and storing eggs

SIZE Eggs are sized according to their weight, from small to jumbo. The most popular size is large, which is the size used for the recipes in this book.

FRESHNESS Eggs are graded AA, A, and B according to the quality of the shell and the thickness and clarity of the whites. Grade AA eggs have clean, unbroken shells, thick whites, and round, bright yolks, and are best for frying or poaching, while grade A eggs are fine for blended eggs and egg dishes. Grade B eggs are typically sold to manufacturers.

STORAGE Always store your eggs in the same carton that you bought them in on a shelf in the refrigerator. The cardboard carton helps eggs retain a proper moisture balance, which adds to their shelf life. Refrigerated, eggs should remain fresh for up to 4 weeks past their sell-by date on the carton. You can also store eggs at a cool room temperature for up to a day or two.

understanding egg carton labels

Purchasing the best-quality eggs from a humane source is often confusing because of the many labels found on cartons. While colorful eggs from local farms are always a treat and probably the freshest you'll find, that's not an option for most of us. Certified organic eggs mean that the hens are fed an organic, vegetarian diet with no antibiotics or pesticides, per official USDA guidelines. They are uncaged, often with access to the outdoors. Free-range hens are uncaged and have some access to the outdoors, but there are no official USDA standards, and this label does not describe the diet of the hens. Certified humane and cage-free labels mean the birds are uncaged indoors, but do not often have access to the outside.

out of the frying pan

perfect fried eggs

From sunny-side up to over hard, fried eggs are a staple of the American breakfast table. And while they might seem intimidating to some, with a few tips on technique, you'll be able to flip an egg without breaking the yolk and cook it to perfection, just like the best short-order cooks.

setting up for success

Before you get started frying an egg, you should first select the appropriate pan. The best pans for frying eggs tend to be those with a nonstick surface, whether a well-seasoned cast iron pan or a good-quality heavy nonstick pan with even heat distribution. Have on hand a wide flat spatula; make sure if you are using a nonstick pan that you use tools designed for nonstick cookware so you don't scratch the surface. Warm the pan over medium heat, add the oil or butter, and let it warm up before adding the eggs. This will help ensure the eggs don't stick.

cracking eggs

Start with cold, fresh eggs that you've pulled directly from the refrigerator. When cold, the yolk stays intact and is more resilient, so you are less likely to break the yolk. Gently tap the center of the egg on a hard, flat surface near the stovetop, such as the kitchen counter. Cracking it on a flat surface helps ensure that stray bits of the shell don't get in the pan.

Holding the cracked egg about an inch over the pan, gently pull the two halves of the shell apart, letting the egg slide into the pan. To make absolutely sure you don't break the yolk or get any stray pieces of shell in the pan, you can crack the egg into a small bowl before sliding it into the pan. If any shell does escape, simply use another piece of shell to remove it.

frying and flipping eggs

Let the egg cook until the white begins to turn opaque, about 2–3 minutes. For a sunny-side up egg, continue cooking until the whites are set, basting gently with the cooking fat (see page 103). For over easy, over medium, or over hard eggs, you'll need to gently flip the egg without breaking the yolk.

To flip the egg, gently slide the spatula under the egg. If you feel any resistance or the egg begins to stick, run the spatula along the edge of the egg until the egg is free of the pan. Cook just until the yolk just begins to set, about 30 seconds more for over easy, 1 minute more for over medium, and 1 1/2 minutes more for over-hard eggs.

a guide to fried eggs

SUNNY-SIDE UP This is quite possibly the simplest method of frying eggs because you don't have to flip them. The clear, bright yellow yolk stays runny while the white is cooked through.

OVER EASY This quick-cooked fried egg is flipped and cooked briefly just to set the white. The yolk remains very runny.

OVER MEDIUM By far the most popular fried egg option, these eggs have a firm white and a slightly runny yolk. They are ideal for perching on top of other components of a dish when you want the yolk to serve as a "sauce."

OVER HARD If you are squeamish about runny yolks, chances are this is the style of egg for you. Also called "over well," this is a good choice for a less messy fried egg sandwich. You can hasten the cooking time by "popping" the yolk with the tip of your spatula and letting it run underneath the whites.

add a fried egg, please

Beyond the classic diner-style breakfast of fried eggs, toast, and hash browns, there are all kinds of delicious ways to use a fried egg:

Make a simple fried egg sandwich by tucking a fried egg between buttered slices of toast.

Top your homemade pizza—especially a simple white pie with olive oil, proscuitto, and herbs—with a few fried eggs.

Top grilled asparagus with a fried egg, then sprinkle with buttery toasted bread crumbs or drizzle with a light vinaigrette.

Gild the lily by topping your burger with a fried egg.

fried eggs with sweet pepper piperade

Pipérade is a Basque-style sauté of sweet onions and colorful peppers, which is great as a side dish but sublime topped with a fried egg. To really take this international dish over the top, serve it with thick slices of pan-fried ham and crusty, toasted bread.

2 tbsp olive oil

1 small onion, thinly sliced

Kosher salt and freshly ground pepper

1 tsp minced garlic

1 red bell pepper, seeded and thinly sliced

1 yellow bell pepper, seeded and thinly sliced

1 orange bell pepper, seeded and thinly sliced

1 tsp sugar

1 tbsp red wine vinegar

2 tbsp butter

4 eggs

2 tbsp chopped fresh flat-leaf (Italian) parsley

Makes 4 servings

Heat a frying pan over medium heat. Add the olive oil, along with the onion and a pinch each of salt and pepper. Cook, stirring occasionally, until the onion just begins to soften, 4–5 minutes. Add the garlic and peppers and a pinch each of salt and pepper. Cook, stirring occasionally, until the peppers are tender with a bit of a bite and the onion is very soft, 6–8 minutes more. Add the sugar and vinegar and continue cooking until the vinegar has almost evaporated, 1–2 minutes more. Cover to keep warm and set aside while you cook the eggs.

Melt the butter in a large nonstick frying pan over medium heat. Crack the eggs into the pan and sprinkle them with salt and pepper. Let the eggs cook until the white begins to turn opaque, 2–3 minutes. If desired, turn the eggs over and cook until the yolk just begins to set, about 30 seconds more.

To serve, divide the pepper mixture between individual plates. Place an egg on top of each serving of peppers, sprinkle with parsley, and serve right away.

egg, bacon, and brie panini

Sweet and chewy bacon, mild and creamy Brie, and peppery arugula are perfect partners in this updated version of the time-honored fried egg sandwich. Great for breakfast, lunch, or even dinner, its savory blend of textures and flavors is sure to please.

½ lb (250 g) bacon

1 loaf ciabatta bread

1 tbsp extra-virgin olive oil, plus extra for brushing

4 oz (110 g) Brie, at room temperature

1 cup (1 oz/30 g) firmly packed baby arugula

4 eggs

Kosher salt and freshly ground pepper

Makes 4 servings

Preheat the oven to 350°F (180°C). Arrange the bacon on a rimmed baking sheet and cook until crisp, turning occasionally, about 20 minutes. Transfer the bacon to paper towels.

Slice the ends off the bread, then cut the bread crosswise into 4 pieces, each about 3–4 inches (7.5–10 cm) wide. Slice each piece in half through the middle, then brush the inside and outside of the bread with olive oil. Spread the Brie on the inside of each top piece of bread, and divide the arugula among the bottom halves of the bread.

Warm the 1 tablespoon olive oil in a large nonstick frying pan over medium heat. Crack the eggs into the pan and sprinkle them with salt and pepper. Let the eggs cook until the white begins to turn opaque, 2–3 minutes. Turn the eggs and continue cooking until the yolks are just set, about 1 minute more. Transfer 1 egg to each sandwich bottom. Divide the bacon evenly on top of the eggs and cover with a top slice of bread.

Heat a cast iron skillet over medium heat. When the pan is hot, add the sandwiches. Cover the sandwiches with a lid, slightly smaller than the top of the pan, and press on the lid gently to flatten the sandwiches. Cook until the bottoms are golden brown, 2–3 minutes. Turn the sandwiches over, press again with the lid, and cook until the cheese has melted and the bread is golden brown on the other side, 2–3 minutes more. Alternatively, cook the sandwiches in a preheated panini press. Serve right away.

steak and eggs

Remember that old-time diner favorite? Here, sautéed mushrooms, fresh thyme, and garlic elevate steak and eggs to a new level. This preparation works with any tender cut of boneless steak, but there's nothing more perfect than a New York strip cooked to a juicy medium-rare.

4 New York strip steaks, about 6 oz (185 g) each

Kosher salt and freshly ground pepper

2 tbsp olive oil

½ lb (250 g) mixed mushrooms, cut into 1-inch (2.5-cm) pieces

½ tsp minced garlic

1 tsp minced fresh thyme

2 tbsp butter

4 eggs

Makes 4 servings

Heat a cast iron frying pan over medium-high heat. Sprinkle the steaks with a generous pinch each of salt and pepper. When the pan is hot, add 1 tablespoon of the olive oil, then the steaks and cook until nicely browned on both sides and medium-rare in the center, about 4 minutes per side. Transfer to a plate and tent with aluminum foil to keep warm.

Add the remaining 1 tablespoon olive oil to the pan and add the mushrooms, garlic, and thyme. Cook, stirring occasionally, until the mushrooms are lightly browned and tender, 4–5 minutes. Sprinkle with salt and pepper and remove from the heat.

While the mushrooms cook, melt the butter in a large nonstick frying pan over medium heat. Crack the eggs into the pan and sprinkle them with salt and pepper. Let the eggs cook until the white begins to turn opaque, 2–3 minutes. If desired, turn the eggs over and cook until the yolk just begins to set, about 30 seconds more.

Place each steak on a plate and add a heaping spoonful of mushrooms. Top each steak with an egg, and serve right away.

corned beef hash and eggs

Because the corned beef takes center stage here, go to your favorite deli and buy a thick piece of the best quality you can get. Better yet, make your own corned beef at home and use the leftovers—its briny salty meat will make the hash even more sensational.

2 tbsp olive oil

4 tbsp (2 oz/60 g) butter

1 large russet potato, peeled and diced into ½-inch (12-mm) pieces

Kosher salt and freshly ground pepper

1 medium onion, diced

3 cups (18 oz/560 g) diced cooked corned beef

2 tbsp chopped fresh flat-leaf (Italian) parsley

4 eggs

Makes 4 servings

Heat a frying pan over medium heat. Add the olive oil and 2 tablespoons of the butter. When the butter has melted, add the potato with a pinch each of salt and pepper. Cook, stirring a few times, until just tender, 5–7 minutes. Add the onion and continue cooking, stirring occasionally, until the onion is soft and translucent and the potato is golden brown, 7–9 minutes more. Add the corned beef and cook, turning over once or twice, just until warmed through, 3–4 minutes more. Stir in the parsley, then taste and adjust the seasoning as needed. Cover and keep warm.

Melt the remaining 2 tablespoons of butter in a large nonstick frying pan over medium heat. Crack the eggs into the pan and sprinkle them with salt and pepper. Let the eggs cook until the whites begin to turn opaque, 2–3 minutes. If desired, turn the eggs over and cook until the yolk just begins to set, about 30 seconds more.

To serve, divide the warm hash between individual plates. Place an egg on top of each mound of hash and serve right away.

toad in the hole

One of many fancifully named traditional English dishes, Toad in the Hole features sausages cooked in Yorkshire pudding batter, which rises to enclose the sausages. This version, also called Eggs in the Basket, marries buttery toast with a hole in the center that cradles a fried egg.

4 tbsp (2 oz/60 g) butter, at room temperature

4 slices whole-wheat bread, or your favorite sliced bread

4 eggs

Kosher salt and freshly ground pepper

Makes 4 servings

Generously butter both sides of the bread, reserving 1–2 teaspoons of butter. Using a 3-inch (7.5-cm) round cutter, cut a circle out of the center of each piece of bread and set aside.

Heat a large nonstick frying pan or griddle over medium heat. Add the reserved butter, spreading it throughout the pan as it melts. When the pan is hot and the butter is melted, place the bread in a single, even layer in the pan, including the cutout circles.

Crack an egg into the hole in each slice of bread and sprinkle lightly with salt and pepper. Let the egg cook until it just begins to turn opaque, about 2–3 minutes, occasionally poking the white to let any uncooked egg fall to the bottom. Slide a spatula under each slice of bread and its egg and carefully turn them over together. Continue to cook until the yolk is still runny but the white is cooked through, about 30 seconds more. Turn the cutout circles as well, cooking until nicely browned on both sides.

Transfer each Toad in the Hole to a plate with a toast round alongside it. Serve right away.

fried eggs with rajas

While uncooked poblano chiles can vary in heat levels, they always turn beautifully sweet when roasted. In Spanish, roasted poblanos are called rajas. The serrano chile adds a spicy kick, and the cream gives a decadent finish. Serve with warmed tortillas or crunchy tortilla chips.

1 tbsp canola oil

1 serrano chile, halved lengthwise, seeded, and thinly sliced

1 small white onion, thinly sliced

Kosher salt and freshly ground pepper

1 tsp minced garlic

8 poblano chiles, roasted (see page 97) and thinly sliced

¼ cup (2 fl oz/60 ml) heavy cream

2 tbsp butter

4 eggs

2 tbsp chopped fresh cilantro

Makes 4 servings

Heat a frying pan over medium heat. Add the canola oil and, when hot, add the serrano chile and the onion with a pinch each of salt and pepper. Cook, stirring occasionally, until the onion is soft and translucent, 6–8 minutes. Stir in the garlic and roasted poblano chiles and cook until fragrant, about 2 minutes more. Add the cream and cook, stirring occasionally, until the mixture is slightly thickened, 2–3 minutes more. Taste and adjust the seasoning as needed with salt and pepper.

Melt the butter in a large nonstick frying pan over medium heat. Crack the eggs into the pan and sprinkle them with salt and pepper. Let the eggs cook until the white begins to turn opaque, 2–3 minutes. If desired, turn the eggs over and cook until the yolk just begins to set, about 30 seconds more.

To serve, divide the chile mixture between individual plates. Place an egg on top of each serving of chiles, sprinkle with cilantro, and serve right away.

omelets and scrambles

creamy, fluffy eggs

Creamy scrambled eggs or a fluffy omelet can be as plain as you like or as decadent as you dare, simply by adding or changing the ingredients. Don't be daunted by scrambles and omelets—with the right tools and techniques, you'll soon be turning them out effortlessly.

setting up for success

Scrambles and omelets are among the quickest and easiest egg dishes you can make, but there are some basic elements for success:

THE PAN Choose a good-quality, heavyweight, nonstick pan that has good heat distribution.

THE SPATULA It's a good idea to have on hand a heatproof rubber spatula, which will help you stir the eggs to achieve the right consistency.

THE FAT Always use oil or butter in the pan even if it is nonstick. The fat will add flavor as well as ensuring the scramble or omelet easily slides out of the pan.

THE HEAT Cook your scramble or omelet slowly over medium heat. While you might be tempted to raise the heat to speed up the process, cooking eggs over high heat can cause them to toughen or overcook.

beating the eggs

For both scrambles and omelets, whole eggs are beaten with a whisk until they are frothy, ideally for at least a minute or two; however, be careful not to overbeat the eggs. Most recipes also call for adding a small amount of milk or water to the eggs to help them retain their moisture, but be sure not to add so much liquid that it makes the eggs watery.

making the perfect scramble

HEAT THE PAN Warm the pan over medium heat, then add oil or butter.

ADD THE EGGS When the oil is warm or the butter melted, reduce the heat to medium-low and add the beaten eggs.

STIR SLOWLY Let the eggs cook undisturbed, until they just begin to set, about 1 minute. Gently stir them with a heatproof rubber spatula, pushing the firmer eggs toward the center of the pan and letting the liquid eggs run to the sides or underneath. For smaller curds, stir more; for large, moist curds, stir slowly and not too often.

ADD THE INGREDIENTS Some ingredients may need to be cooked before you add the eggs. Add any additional ingredients you are using after the eggs set.

REMOVE THE PAN FROM THE HEAT The eggs will continue to cook off the heat, so pull them off the stove top just before they are done.

making the perfect omelet

PREPARE THE EGGS Follow the steps above to warm the pan, add the eggs, and stir the eggs while cooking, keeping them in an even layer.

ADD THE INGREDIENTS When the eggs are set in an even layer and there is no more standing liquid, scatter any additional ingredients you are using, such as cheese, vegetables, or meat, over the top.

FOLD THE OMELET Using your spatula, carefully fold the omelet in half or into thirds. Larger omelets should be folded in half, while thinner omelets, using fewer eggs, should be folded into thirds.

breakfast for dinner

Savory scrambles and omelets are favorites at the breakfast table, where they are often served with home-fried potatoes or hash browns and buttery toast. But they also make for a deliciously nutritious and simple lunch or supper. To make a scramble or an omelet into a meal, serve it with a fresh mixed green salad tossed with a light vinaigrette. Add complimentary ingredients to the salad, depending upon what you've added to your eggs. For example, serve the Pesto Scrambled Eggs with a fresh tomato, Parmesan, and arugula salad.

classic herb omelet

These simple yet flavorful French-inspired omelets are prepared one at a time and cook up ultrathin, almost like crepes. Served with a fresh mixed green salad and a glass of dry white wine, they are perfect for a light summer lunch, Parisian style.

8 eggs

Kosher salt and freshly ground pepper

1 tbsp minced fresh flat-leaf (Italian) parsley

1 tbsp minced fresh chives

2 tsp minced fresh tarragon

4 tbsp (2 oz/60 g) butter

Makes 4 servings

In a bowl, whisk together the eggs, 1 tablespoon water, and a pinch each of salt and pepper. Add the parsley, chives, and tarragon and continue whisking until the eggs are nice and frothy.

Melt 1 tablespoon of the butter in a small nonstick frying pan over medium heat. Pour in one-quarter of the egg mixture. Cook until the eggs just begin to set, about 1 minute. Using a heatproof rubber spatula, gently stir the eggs around the pan, letting any uncooked egg run onto the bottom of the pan. When no more raw egg is visible, stop stirring and let the eggs cook gently until set. Gently loosen the edges of the omelet with the spatula, then, using the spatula, fold the two opposite sides toward the middle to fold the omelet into thirds.

Slide the omelet onto an individual plate and serve right away. Repeat the cooking process with the remaining eggs and butter.

ham and cheddar omelet

Filled with smoky ham and tangy melted Cheddar, this hearty omelet is a classic American breakfast staple. Have fun adding more of your favorite ingredients, such as blanched asparagus or spinach, or diced and sautéed onions and bell peppers.

8 eggs

Kosher salt and freshly ground pepper

2 tbsp butter

1 cup (6 oz/185 g) diced country ham

½ cup (2 oz/60 g) coarsely grated sharp Cheddar cheese

Makes 4 servings

In a bowl, whisk together the eggs, 1 tablespoon water, and a pinch each of salt and pepper. Continue whisking until the eggs are nice and frothy.

Melt the butter in a 12-inch (30-cm) nonstick frying pan over medium-high heat. Pour in the egg mixture cook until the eggs just begin to set, about 1 minute. Using a heatproof rubber spatula, gently stir the eggs around the pan, letting any uncooked egg run onto the bottom of the pan. When no more raw egg is visible, stop stirring and let the eggs cook until set. Sprinkle the ham and Cheddar over the top then, using a spatula, gently fold the omelet in half. Use the spatula to slide the omelet onto a warmed serving platter, cut crosswise into 4 pieces, and serve right away.

curried eggs

This distinctively Indian take on scrambled eggs is rich with warm spices, and delicious served with a cool cucumber–yogurt sauce. To pull out all the stops for a special brunch, serve it spooned over warmed Indian flatbread, along with mango lassis.

½ tsp Indian-style curry powder

½ tsp ground cumin

½ tsp ground coriander

½ cup (4 oz/125 g) Greek-style plain yogurt

½ small English cucumber, seeded and finely diced

1 tsp freshly squeezed lemon juice

Kosher salt and freshly ground pepper

8 eggs

2 tbsp milk

1½ tbsp butter

Makes 4 servings

Place the curry powder, cumin, and coriander in a small, dry frying pan over medium heat. Toast the spices, stirring occasionally, until fragrant, about 1 minute. Transfer the spices to a dish and set aside.

In a small bowl, combine the yogurt, cucumber, lemon juice, and a pinch each of salt and pepper. Set aside.

In a bowl, whisk together the eggs, milk, spice mixture, and a pinch each of salt and pepper. Continue whisking until the eggs are nice and frothy.

Melt the butter in a nonstick frying pan over medium-low heat. Add the eggs and let cook until they just begin to set, about 1 minute. Using a heatproof rubber spatula, gently push the eggs around the pan, letting any uncooked egg run onto the bottom of the pan. Stir gently, cooking until the eggs have set, about 2–3 minutes total. Transfer the eggs to a warmed serving platter, and serve with the cucumber yogurt sauce on the side.

cowboy eggs

This hearty scramble contains everything you crave in a rib-sticking breakfast, such as pan-fried potatoes and ham, creamy scrambled eggs, and zingy pepper jack cheese. Feel free to substitute bacon, sausage, or Mexican-style chorizo for the ham.

1 tbsp extra-virgin olive oil

2 tbsp butter

1 medium russet potato, peeled and finely diced

Kosher salt and freshly ground pepper

¾ cup (4½ oz/140 g) diced country ham

8 eggs

2 tbsp milk

½ cup (2 oz/60 g) coarsely grated pepper jack cheese

2 tbsp minced fresh chives

Makes 4 servings

Heat the olive oil and butter in a nonstick frying pan over medium heat. When the butter has melted, add the potato with a pinch each of salt and pepper. Cook, stirring a few times, until the potato is tender and lightly browned, 7–9 minutes. Add the ham and cook, stirring occasionally, until lightly browned, 1–2 minutes more.

Meanwhile, in a bowl, whisk together the eggs, milk, and a pinch each of salt and pepper. Continue whisking until the eggs are nice and frothy.

When the potato and ham are cooked, reduce the heat to medium-low. Add the eggs and let cook until they just begin to set, about 1 minute. Using a heatproof rubber spatula, gently push the eggs around the pan, letting any uncooked egg run onto the bottom of the pan. Stir in the pepper jack cheese and chives. Continue cooking, stirring occasionally, until the eggs have set and the cheese has melted, 2–3 minutes more. Transfer to a warmed serving platter and serve right away.

salami and arugula scramble

This simple scramble is packed with the salty flavor of salami and the peppery bite of fresh arugula. Look for good-quality artisanal salami, which you can find at many Italian delis. Serve this elegant Italian-style egg dish with thick, buttery slices of toasted Italian bread.

1 tsp canola oil

¼ lb (125 g) good-quality salami, diced

8 eggs

2 tbsp milk

Kosher salt and freshly ground pepper

1½ tbsp butter

1 cup (1 oz/30 g) firmly packed baby arugula

Makes 4 servings

Warm the canola oil in a nonstick frying pan over medium heat. Add the salami and cook, stirring occasionally, until browned in spots, 3–4 minutes.

Meanwhile, in a bowl, whisk together the eggs, milk, and a pinch each of salt and pepper. Continue whisking until the eggs are nice and frothy

When the salami is well browned, reduce the heat to medium-low and add the butter. When the butter has melted, add the eggs and let cook until they just begin to set, about 1 minute. Using a heatproof rubber spatula, gently stir the eggs around the pan, letting any uncooked egg run onto the bottom of the pan. When the eggs are about half cooked, 1–2 minutes more, stir in the arugula. Stir gently, cooking until the eggs have set, about 1 minute more. Transfer the eggs to a warmed serving platter and serve right away.

garden scramble

When your farmers' market is abundant with summer's delicate zucchini and ripe, juicy tomatoes, add them to this fresh and easy scramble. To make the scramble even more beautiful, mix it up with multicolored heirloom tomatoes and striped or yellow zucchini.

8 eggs

2 tbsp milk

Kosher salt and freshly ground pepper

1½ tbsp butter

1 small zucchini, finely diced

1 medium tomato, seeded and diced

1 cup (1 oz/30 g) firmly packed baby spinach

¼ cup (1 oz/30 g) freshly grated *pecorino romano* cheese, plus more for serving

Makes 4 servings

In a bowl, whisk together the eggs, milk, and a pinch each of salt and pepper. Continue whisking until the eggs are nice and frothy.

Melt the butter in a nonstick frying pan over medium heat. Add the zucchini with a pinch of salt. Cook, stirring, until just tender, about 1 minute. Add the tomato and stir to combine. Reduce the heat to medium-low, add the eggs, and let cook until they just begin to set, about 1 minute. Using a heatproof rubber spatula, gently push the eggs around the pan, letting any uncooked egg run onto the bottom of the pan. When the eggs are about half cooked, 1–2 minutes more, stir in the spinach and *pecorino romano*. Stir gently to combine and continue cooking until the eggs have set, about 1 minute more.

Transfer the eggs to a warmed serving platter, sprinkle with more cheese, and serve right away.

pesto scrambled eggs

The basil pesto in this recipe is a snap to make, but if you've already got store-bought pesto in the fridge, by all means use it here. These "green eggs" would, of course, be great with a thick slice of ham, or, for a fresh summer brunch, serve them with slices of ripe tomato.

1 cup (1 oz/30 g) gently packed fresh basil, plus about 5 reserved leaves for garnish

1 small clove garlic, chopped

2 tbsp pine nuts, toasted

¼ cup (2 fl oz/60 ml) extra-virgin olive oil

Kosher salt and freshly ground pepper

8 eggs

2 tbsp milk

1½ tbsp butter

¼ cup (1 oz/30 g) freshly grated Parmesan cheese

1 piece Parmesan cheese, about 1 oz (30 g)

Makes 4 servings

To make the pesto, place the basil, garlic, and pine nuts in a food processor. Pulse until the mixture is coarsely chopped. With the motor running, add the olive oil until the pesto is smooth. Remove the pesto from the processor and season to taste with salt and pepper. Set aside.

In a bowl, whisk together the eggs, milk, and a pinch each of salt and pepper. Continue whisking until the eggs are nice and frothy.

Melt the butter in a nonstick frying pan over medium-low heat. Add the eggs and let cook until they just begin to set, about 1 minute. Gently stir in the pesto. Using a heatproof rubber spatula, gently stir the eggs around the pan, letting any uncooked egg run onto the bottom of the pan. When the eggs are about half cooked, 1–2 minutes more, stir in the grated Parmesan cheese. Stir gently, cooking until the eggs have set and the cheese has melted, about 1 minute more.

Transfer the eggs to a warm serving platter. Tear the reserved basil leaves over the top and, using a vegetable peeler, cut a few shavings from the piece of Parmesan cheese over the eggs. Serve right away.

chorizo and green chile scramble

Here, chorizo lends spiciness and roasted chiles add a mild but distinctive heat. Look for uncured Mexican-style chorizo sausages seasoned with paprika, garlic, and cayenne. For an extra kick, top this south-of-the-border scramble with a few dashes of your favorite hot sauce.

1 tbsp canola oil

½ lb (250 g) Mexican-style (uncooked) chorizo, casings removed

8 eggs

2 tbsp milk

Kosher salt and freshly ground pepper

1½ tbsp butter

3 poblano chiles, roasted (see page 97) and finely chopped

2 cloves garlic, roasted (see page 97) and minced

2 tbsp chopped fresh cilantro

Makes 4 servings

Heat the canola oil in a nonstick frying pan over medium heat. Add the chorizo, using a wooden spoon to break it into bite-size pieces. Cook, stirring occasionally, until lightly browned and cooked through, 5–6 minutes. Using a slotted spoon, transfer the chorizo to paper towels. Discard any fat in the pan.

Meanwhile, in a bowl, whisk together the eggs, milk, and a pinch each of salt and pepper. Continue whisking until the eggs are nice and frothy.

Return the pan to medium-low heat and melt the butter. Add the eggs and let cook until they just begin to set, about 1 minute. Add the chorizo, poblano chiles, and garlic. Using a heatproof rubber spatula, gently stir the eggs around the pan, letting any uncooked egg run onto the bottom of the pan. Stir gently, cooking until the eggs have set, about 2–3 minutes more.

Transfer the eggs to a warmed serving platter or individual plates, sprinkle with cilantro, and serve right away.

creamy scrambled eggs with smoked salmon

Smoked salmon, cream cheese, onion, and chives—all your favorite bagel toppings are folded into these silky scrambled eggs. For a heartier meal, serve over toasted bagel halves, and for a special occasion or holiday brunch, add a heaping spoonful of luxurious salmon roe.

1 tsp canola oil

½ small red onion, finely diced

Kosher salt and freshly ground pepper

8 eggs

2 tbsp milk

1½ tbsp butter

¼ lb (125 g) cold-smoked salmon, cut into thin strips

2 oz (60 g) cream cheese, cut into small pieces

2 tbsp finely minced fresh chives

Makes 4 servings

Heat the canola oil in a nonstick frying pan over medium heat. Add the onion with a pinch each of salt and pepper and cook, stirring occasionally, until soft and translucent, 6–8 minutes.

Meanwhile, in a bowl, whisk together the eggs and milk until the eggs are nice and frothy.

When the onion is ready, reduce the heat to medium-low and add the butter. When the butter has melted, add the eggs and let cook until they just begin to set, about 1 minute. Add the salmon. Using a heatproof rubber spatula, gently stir the eggs around the pan, letting any uncooked egg run onto the bottom of the pan. When the eggs are about half cooked, about 1 minute more, stir in the cream cheese. Stir gently until the eggs have set and the cheese has melted, about 1 minute more. Season to taste with salt and pepper if needed.

Transfer the eggs to a warmed serving platter, sprinkle with the chives, and serve right away.

frittatas

all about frittatas

A snap to make and chock-full of fresh vegetables, herbs, cheeses, and meats—in as many combinations as you can imagine—a frittata is simply a quiche without its crust. It is delicious served both warm and at room temperature, making it perfect for a picnic or a party.

what is a frittata?

A frittata is often described as a quiche minus the crust or an Italian version of an omelet. But unlike its French cousin, which carefully folds the egg around the filling, the frittata mixes the filling with the eggs and cooks them together in a large pancake. Plump and golden, it shows how a few eggs, a handful of vegetables, and a sprinkling of cheese can become a simple yet hearty meal to start the day.

Frittatas can be as casual or dressed up as you want them to be—they can be served directly out of the pan, or transferred to a platter and garnished with herbs, vegetables, or cheese for a more sophisticated presentation.

before you start cooking

Before you get started making your frittata, read through all the steps of the recipe, then determine how you want to serve it. This will enable you to choose the most appropriate pan.

COOKING A FRITTATA The recipes here direct you to start the frittata on the stovetop and finish cooking it in the oven or under the broiler. You can also cook the entire frittata on the stovetop, by flipping it out onto a plate and sliding it back into the pan to cook on the other side, or by using a frittata pan designed for stovetop use.

IN THE PAN OR ON THE PLATTER The next step is to determine whether you want to serve your frittata directly from the pan or transfer it to a serving platter. Serving it from the pan is a nice, casual option for a simple family breakfast, while serving it on the platter makes it a bit more special for the holidays or when you have company.

WHICH PAN IS BEST? If you are cooking a frittata using the stovetop-to-oven method, and serving directly from the pan, you could use a well-seasoned cast iron pan. If you are cooking the frittata using the stovetop-to-oven method, and plan to transfer it to a platter, use a good-quality nonstick ovenproof pan. For cooking the frittata entirely on the stovetop, you can use a pan specifically made for frittatas, which consist of two nonstick pans that have interlocking handles. This enables you to flip the frittata on the stovetop to cook both sides, rather than putting it in the oven.

personalizing your frittata

Frittatas, like their quiche and omelet cousins, offer a wealth of variations depending upon the combination of ingredients that you choose to fill them with (see page 98 for filling ideas). Once you've mastered the many delicious recipes in this chapter, start experimenting with other ingredients.

To personalize your frittata, simply follow one of the recipes in this chapter, but mix and match your own favorite ingredients by substituting them for what is called for in the recipe. Select two or more ingredients, such as a vegetable, herb, meat, and cheese in any combination. When you are choosing ingredients, keep in mind which vegetables and herbs are in season, and select the best-quality meats and cheeses you can find.

fun with frittatas

The best thing about a frittata is that you can have fun with the ingredients you fill it with, as well as how you serve it.

A frittata can be made in advance and is delicious at room temperature, so it makes for great party fare. And while it is typically cut into wedges, you can also cut it into smaller bite-sized pieces.

Adding a garnish will give your frittata a bit of elegance and freshness. Once on the serving platter, add a sprinkle of chopped fresh herbs or some of the other ingredients found in the frittata, such as cherry tomatoes or feta cheese.

cherry tomato, mozzarella, and basil frittata

A flawless caprese salad meets a fluffy frittata in this Italian-inspired dish. Sweet tomatoes, creamy mozzarella, and fresh basil are all at their best in this delicious ode to summer, which is perfect for a late brunch, a midday picnic, or an early supper al fresco.

½ bunch fresh basil leaves, about ½ cup (½ oz/15 g)

1 cup (6 oz/190 g) cherry tomatoes, halved

¼ lb (125 g) fresh whole-milk mozzarella cheese, diced

Kosher salt and freshly ground pepper

10 eggs

1 tbsp cream or milk

1 tbsp extra-virgin olive oil

Makes 4–6 servings

Preheat the oven to 425°F (220°C). Reserve about 2 tablespoons of the basil leaves and cut the remaining leaves into thin ribbons. Transfer the cut basil to a bowl and add the tomatoes, mozzarella, and a pinch each of salt and pepper. Stir well and set aside for 10 minutes.

In a bowl, whisk together the eggs, cream, and a pinch each of salt and pepper.

Warm the olive oil in a 10-inch (25-cm) ovenproof nonstick frying pan over medium-low heat. Add the egg mixture and cook, stirring gently, until the eggs begin to set but do not begin to scramble. Gently stir in the tomato-mozzarella mixture. Cook the eggs, undisturbed, until they begin to set around the edges, 2–3 minutes more. Transfer the frying pan to the oven and bake until the eggs are set around the edges and just firm in the center, about 5 minutes more.

Loosen the sides of the frittata with a spatula and hold a platter over the top of the pan. Holding the sides with hot pads, invert the frittata onto the platter. Cut into wedges, garnish with the reserved basil, and serve warm or at room temperature.

bacon, mushroom, and sweet onion frittata

When you're looking for comfort food for breakfast, this frittata will satisfy even the most voracious appetite. Even better, the mouth-watering combination of salty bacon, sweet onions, and earthy mushrooms are items you are likely to have on hand. Serve it with warm biscuits.

½ lb (250 g) bacon, cut crosswise into ½-inch strips

1 tbsp extra-virgin olive oil

½ sweet onion, diced

Kosher salt and freshly ground pepper

½ lb (250 g) cremini or button mushrooms, brushed clean and sliced

10 eggs

1 tbsp cream or milk

1 tsp minced fresh thyme

Makes 4–6 servings

Preheat the oven to 425°F (220°C). In a 10-inch (25-cm) ovenproof nonstick frying pan over medium heat, cook the bacon, stirring occasionally, until crisp, about 10 minutes. Using a slotted spoon, transfer the bacon to paper towels. Pour off all but 1 teaspoon of the bacon fat.

Add the olive oil to the pan and return it to medium heat. Stir in the onion with a pinch each of salt and pepper and cook until it just begins to soften, about 5 minutes. Stir in the mushrooms with a pinch each of salt and pepper. Continue cooking until the onion is soft and translucent and the mushrooms are tender, 4–6 minutes more, stirring occasionally.

Meanwhile, in a bowl, whisk together the eggs, cream, thyme, and a pinch each of salt and pepper.

When the onion and mushrooms are done, reduce the heat to medium-low. Add the egg mixture and the bacon and cook, stirring gently, until the eggs begin to set but do not begin to scramble. Cook the eggs, undisturbed, until they begin to set around the edges, 2–3 minutes more. Transfer the frying pan to the oven and bake until the eggs are set around the edges and just firm in the center, about 5 minutes more.

Loosen the sides of the frittata with a spatula and hold a platter over the top of the pan. Holding the sides with hot pads, invert the frittata onto the platter. Cut into wedges and serve warm or at room temperature.

zucchini, tomato, and cheddar frittata

Chock-full of vegetables, this simple, summer-inspired frittata uses the bounty of the season's best produce. When they are in season, use multicolored heirloom tomatoes, yellow crookneck squash, and pattypan squash fresh from your local farmers' market.

10 eggs

½ cup (2 oz/60 g) sharp Cheddar cheese

1 tbsp cream or milk

1 tsp minced fresh marjoram

Kosher salt and freshly ground pepper

1 tbsp extra-virgin olive oil

1 medium zucchini, diced

2 medium tomatoes, diced

Makes 4–6 servings

Preheat the oven to 425°F (220°C). In a bowl, whisk together the eggs, Cheddar, cream, marjoram, and a pinch each of salt and pepper.

Warm the olive oil in a 10-inch (25-cm) ovenproof nonstick frying pan over medium heat. When the pan is hot, add the zucchini with a pinch of salt. Cook, stirring, until just tender, about 1 minute. Add the tomatoes and stir to combine. Reduce the heat to medium-low and add the egg mixture. Cook, stirring gently, until the eggs begin to set but do not begin to scramble. Cook the eggs, undisturbed, until they begin to set around the edges, 2–3 minutes more. Transfer the frying pan to the oven and bake until the eggs are set around the edges and just firm in the center, about 5 minutes more.

Loosen the sides of the frittata with a spatula and hold a platter over the top of the pan. Holding the sides with hot pads, invert the frittata onto the platter. Cut into wedges and serve warm or at room temperature.

potato, goat cheese, and dill frittata

The combination of dill and goat cheese gives this frittata a decidedly savory flavor, making it ideal for a simple lunch. The potatoes add substance, but be sure to slice them very thinly—a mandoline or a v–slicer works well—so that they cook through.

10 eggs

⅓ cup (1½ oz/50 g) soft goat cheese, crumbled into small pieces

2 tbsp finely chopped fresh dill, plus small sprigs for garnish

1 tbsp cream or milk

Kosher salt and freshly ground pepper

1 tbsp extra–virgin olive oil

1 medium russet potato, peeled and very thinly sliced

Makes 4—6 servings

Preheat the oven to 425°F (220°C). In a bowl, whisk together the eggs, goat cheese, 2 tablespoons dill, cream, and a pinch each of salt and pepper.

Warm the olive oil in a 10-inch (25-cm) ovenproof nonstick frying pan over medium heat. Add the potato and cook, stirring gently and occasionally, until tender and lightly browned, 7–9 minutes. Reduce the heat to medium-low and add the egg mixture. Cook, stirring gently, until the eggs begin to set but do not begin to scramble. Cook the eggs, undisturbed, until they begin to set around the edges, 2–3 minutes more. Transfer the frying pan to the oven and bake until the eggs are set around the edges and just firm in the center, about 5 minutes more.

Loosen the sides of the frittata with a spatula and hold a platter over the top of the pan. Holding the sides with hot pads, invert the frittata onto the platter. Cut into wedges, garnish with the dill sprigs, and serve warm or at room temperature.

roasted red pepper and potato frittata

This hearty frittata, studded with tender potatoes and roasted peppers, is perfect at any time of day. Roasting the peppers mellows their flavor and concentrates their sweetness. They can be roasted a few days in advance; just cover them with olive oil and refrigerate until needed.

10 eggs

2 tbsp chopped cilantro leaves, plus more for garnish

1 tbsp cream or milk

Kosher salt and freshly ground pepper

1 tbsp extra-virgin olive oil

1 medium russet potato, peeled and diced

1 medium onion, diced

2 roasted red bell peppers (page 97), seeded and chopped

Makes 4–6 servings

Preheat the oven to 425°F (220°C). In a bowl, whisk together the eggs, 2 tablespoons cilantro, cream, and a pinch each of salt and pepper.

Warm the olive oil in a 10-inch (25-cm) ovenproof nonstick frying pan over medium heat. Add the potato with a pinch each of salt and pepper and cook, stirring occasionally, until just tender, 5–6 minutes. Add the onion with a pinch of salt and continue cooking, stirring occasionally, until the potato is golden brown and the onion is soft and translucent, 4–5 minutes more. Stir in the chopped bell peppers, and season to taste, if needed.

Reduce the heat to medium-low and add the egg mixture. Cook, stirring gently, until the eggs begin to set but do not begin to scramble. Cook the eggs, undisturbed, until they begin to set around the edges, 2–3 minutes more. Transfer the frying pan to the oven and bake until the eggs are set around the edges and just firm in the center, about 5 minutes more.

Loosen the sides of the frittata with a spatula and hold a platter over the top of the pan. Holding the sides with hot pads, invert the frittata onto the platter. Cut into wedges, garnish with the remaining cilantro, and serve warm or at room temperature.

spinach, tomato, and feta frittata

Fresh ripe tomatoes, salty feta cheese, and aromatic oregano are classic Greek ingredients, and make for a flavorful frittata that is sure to become a family favorite. Delicious warm, the bright flavors of this classic frittata are just as good at room temperature.

10 eggs

1 tbsp cream or milk

2 tsp minced fresh oregano, plus more for garnish (optional)

Kosher salt and freshly ground pepper

1 tbsp extra-virgin olive oil

2 medium tomatoes, diced, plus more for garnish (optional)

½ cup (2½ oz/75 g) feta cheese, crumbled, plus more for garnish (optional)

1½ cups (1½ oz/45 g) firmly packed baby spinach

Makes 4–6 servings

Preheat the oven to 425°F (220°C). In a bowl, whisk together the eggs, cream, 2 teaspoons oregano, and a pinch each of salt and pepper.

Warm the olive oil in a 10-inch (25-cm) ovenproof nonstick frying pan over medium-low heat. Add the egg mixture and cook, stirring gently, until the eggs begin to set but do not begin to scramble. Gently stir in the 2 diced tomatoes, the ½ cup feta, and the spinach. Cook the eggs, undisturbed, until they begin to set around the edges, 2–3 minutes more. Transfer the frying pan to the oven and bake until the eggs are set around the edges and just firm in the center, about 5 minutes more.

Loosen the sides of the frittata with a spatula and hold a platter over the top of the pan. Holding the sides with hot pads, invert the frittata onto the platter. If desired, garnish the frittata with extra diced tomatoes, oregano, and feta. Cut into wedges and serve warm or at room temperature.

artichoke, red pepper, and sausage frittata

From North Africa, merguez is a spicy lamb sausage, highly seasoned and full of bold flavors, such as sumac for tartness and cayenne pepper, harissa, or paprika for heat. If you cannot find merguez, you may substitute another spicy, fresh sausage, such as hot Italian links.

1 tsp plus 1 tbsp extra-virgin olive oil

½ lb (250 g) *merguez* sausages, casings removed

2 fresh, jarred, or frozen artichoke bottoms, thinly sliced (page 97)

Kosher salt and freshly ground pepper

1 red bell pepper, seeded and diced

8 eggs

1 tbsp cream or milk

Makes 4–6 servings

Preheat the oven to 425°F (220°C). Warm the 1 teaspoon olive oil in a 10-inch (25-cm) ovenproof nonstick frying pan over medium heat. Add the sausage and, using a wooden spoon, break it into bite-size pieces. Cook, stirring, until lightly browned, 5–6 minutes. Using a slotted spoon, transfer the sausage to paper towels. Discard all but 1 tablespoon of the fat.

Return the pan to the heat and add the artichokes with a pinch each of salt and pepper. Cook, stirring, until lightly golden, 3–4 minutes for fresh, or about 1 minute for jarred or frozen. Add the bell pepper and continue to cook, stirring occasionally, until the artichoke is tender and the bell pepper has softened, 3–4 minutes more. Return the sausage to the pan and stir to combine. Remove the pan from the heat.

In a bowl, whisk together the eggs, cream, and a pinch of salt and pepper. Return the pan to medium-low heat and add the remaining 1 tablespoon olive oil. Add the egg mixture and cook, stirring gently, until the eggs begin to set but do not begin to scramble. Cook the eggs, undisturbed, until they begin to set around the edges, 2–3 minutes more. Transfer the frying pan to the oven and bake until the eggs are set around the edges and just firm in the center, about 5 minutes more.

Loosen the sides of the frittata with a spatula and hold a platter over the top of the pan. Holding the sides with hot pads, invert the frittata onto the platter. Cut into wedges and serve warm or at room temperature.

pancetta, chard, and parmesan frittata

Cut into bite-size squares, this Italian frittata is fantastic served on a colorful antipasto platter alongside cured meats, such as salami; cheeses, such as fresh mozzarella; marinated olives, artichokes, red bell peppers, and mushrooms; and plenty of toasted crostini.

8 eggs

1 tbsp cream or milk

Kosher salt and freshly ground pepper

2 oz (60 g) pancetta, diced

1 lb (500 g) Swiss chard, stems finely diced and leaves chopped

1 tbsp extra-virgin olive oil

2 tbsp pine nuts, toasted

⅓ cup (1½ oz/45 g) freshly grated Parmesan cheese

1 piece Parmesan cheese, about 1 oz (30 g)

Makes 4–6 servings

Preheat the oven to 425°F (220°C). In a bowl, whisk together the eggs, cream, and a pinch each of salt and pepper.

In a 10-inch (25-cm) ovenproof nonstick frying pan over medium heat, cook the pancetta, stirring occasionally, until the pancetta begins to brown and render some fat, 2–3 minutes. Add the chard stems and cook, stirring occasionally, until tender, 2–4 minutes more. Add the chard leaves with a pinch each of salt and pepper, stir well, cover the pan, and cook until the leaves begin to wilt, 2–3 minutes. Remove the cover and stir the chard mixture well, continuing to cook until the leaves are wilted and most of the moisture has evaporated, about 2 minutes more.

Reduce the heat to medium-low and add the olive oil. Add the egg mixture and pine nuts and cook, stirring gently, until the eggs begin to set but do not begin to scramble. When the eggs just begin to set, gently stir in the grated Parmesan. Cook the eggs, undisturbed, until they begin to set around the edges, 2–3 minutes more. Transfer the frying pan to the oven and bake until the eggs are set around the edges and just firm in the center, about 5 minutes more.

Loosen the sides of the frittata with a spatula and hold a platter over the top of the pan. Holding the sides with hot pads, invert the frittata onto the platter. Using a vegetable peeler, cut a few shavings from the piece of Parmesan cheese over the top. Serve warm or at room temperature.

crab, pea, and ricotta frittata

Sweet, fresh crabmeat, creamy ricotta, and tender English peas make this an elegant spring frittata worthy of serving company. For a further touch of polish, add sliced, toasted brioche to the plate. Frozen peas will work in a pinch; just thaw them a bit before they go into the eggs.

1 cup (5 oz/155 g) shelled fresh English peas, about 1 lb (500 g) unshelled

10 eggs

1 tbsp cream or milk

Kosher salt and freshly ground pepper

1 tbsp extra-virgin olive oil

½ lb (250 g) fresh lump crabmeat, picked over for shell fragments

½ cup (4 oz/125 g) ricotta cheese

1 tbsp chopped fresh chives, for garnish

Makes 4–6 servings

Bring a saucepan of generously salted water to a boil. Add the peas and cook until just tender, about 2 minutes. Drain the peas and immediately plunge them into a bowl of ice water. When cool, drain the peas again, pat dry, and set aside.

Preheat the oven to 425°F (220°C). In a bowl, whisk together the eggs, cream, and a pinch each of salt and pepper.

Warm the olive oil in a 10-inch (25-cm) ovenproof nonstick frying pan over medium-low heat. Add the egg mixture and cook, stirring gently, until the eggs begin to set but do not begin to scramble. Gently stir in the peas and crabmeat. Cook the eggs, undisturbed, until they begin to set around the edges, 2–3 minutes more. Dollop the ricotta cheese evenly over the top of the frittata. Transfer the frying pan to the oven and bake until the eggs are set around the edges and just firm in the center, about 5 minutes more.

Loosen the sides of the frittata with a spatula and hold a platter over the top of the pan. Holding the sides with hot pads, invert the frittata onto the platter. Cut into wedges, garnish with the chives, and serve warm or at room temperature.

baked egg dishes

quiches, stratas, and more

When you want to make something special for brunch, there are few dishes more impressive or comforting than quiches, stratas, and baked egg dishes. From classic quiche Lorraine to whimsical eggs baked in prosciutto nests, you will surely dazzle your guests with these recipes.

getting started

Baked egg dishes include a wide spectrum of recipes, from creamy quiches and hearty stratas to savory eggs baked in ramekins and individual egg tarts. Some of these recipes take a little more time or attention than scrambles or other simple egg dishes, but they are well worth the effort, especially when entertaining friends and family. And while each of these recipes is appropriate for a special breakfast or brunch, they are equally delicious as a main course for lunch or even a light supper.

what you'll need

While you don't need specialized equipment to make these recipes, you will need more than a frying pan. The quiche recipes in this book can all be made in a 10-inch (25-cm) deep tart pan or an 11-inch (28-cm) pie or quiche pan; most of the baked egg dishes call for ½-cup (4 fl oz/125 ml) ramekins or custard cups; and the tartlets require eight 4½-inch (11.5-cm) tartlet pans or flan rings. The stratas can be baked in standard-sized baking dishes.

when is it done?

The best custard-based baked egg dishes—such as quiches and stratas—should be light and creamy, never dense or curdled. To ensure success, it's important to cook custard-based dishes at a low oven temperature so they don't overcook. Test for doneness by gently shaking the pan; the custard should have a slight jiggle. Also, a wooden skewer inserted into the custard should come out clean but moist. Make sure to remove the dish from the oven and let it rest for at least 10 minutes before you cut into it.

the perfect crust

Making homemade pastry crust for your quiche or tarts doesn't have to be intimidating. In fact, if you plan ahead, it can be quick and easy. And truly, a homemade crust is half of what makes a quiche or tart so endearing.

Here are a few tips to help you make the perfect crust:

KEEP YOUR INGREDIENTS COLD Keeping the butter cold is essential to a flaky crust, because you don't want the butter to completely combine with the dough. You can even use frozen butter to be sure it remains chilled. Also, using cold water helps keep the butter and the dough cold.

WORK QUICKLY Don't panic, but do try to work quickly. Making your dough in a food processor or stand mixer will help you work faster; these tools also help keep your warm hands out of the dough, keeping it cold.

DON'T OVERWORK IT When cutting the butter into the flour, make sure your butter remains about the size of small peas. Once you've lightly mixed the dough together, dump it out onto a work surface and gently knead it into a ball. It should be rough with streaks of butter running through it.

PLAN AHEAD Pastry dough freezes well, so make it in advance and store it in the freezer. Or make a double batch to have on hand whenever you want to prepare a quiche at a moment's notice.

a festive meal

Baked egg dishes are ideal for holiday entertaining or get-togethers, as they are not only impressive, but most can be prepped or prepared in advance. Quiches are ideal for a buffet as they can be served hot or at room temperature, and stratas are perfect for feeding a crowd. For a more intimate brunch or lunch, individual egg tarts or baked eggs in ramekins are elegant and delicious.

These savory dishes lend themselves well to fresh side dishes such as mixed green salad tossed with vinaigrette or sliced ripe tomatoes, along with a basket of breads or muffins.

quiche lorraine

Traditional and very French, this decadent quiche is rich with cream, bacon, and Gruyère cheese. Because there are only a few ingredients it's important to use the best-quality bacon and cheese you can find. Toss a crisp green salad while the quiche is resting, and enjoy.

1 prebaked deep tart or pie shell (page 95)

¾ lb (375 g) good-quality thick-sliced bacon, cut crosswise into ½-inch (12-mm) pieces

6 eggs

1½ cups (12 fl oz/ 375 ml) whole milk

1½ cups (12 fl oz/ 375 ml) heavy cream

⅛ tsp freshly grated nutmeg

Kosher salt and freshly ground pepper

1 cup (4 oz/125 g) coarsely grated Gruyère cheese

Makes 6–8 servings

Preheat the oven to 375°F (190°C). Prepare the tart or pie shell and prebake as directed. In a frying pan over medium heat, cook the bacon, stirring occasionally, until crisp, about 10 minutes. Using a slotted spoon, transfer the bacon to paper towels.

In a bowl, whisk together the eggs, milk, cream, nutmeg, and a pinch each of salt and pepper. Stir in the bacon and cheese. Pour the mixture into the tart shell. Bake the quiche until golden on top and just barely jiggling in the center, 45–50 minutes.

Cool the quiche on a rack for at least 20 minutes before slicing. Cut into wedges and serve warm or at room temperature.

baked egg dishes

asparagus and leek quiche

The appearance of asparagus and leeks in the farmers' markets is a harbinger of spring, and what better way to showcase those delicately flavored vegetables than tucked into a creamy quiche with buttery, flaky pastry. A simply dressed frisée salad would be just right alongside.

1 prebaked deep tart or pie shell (page 95)

½ lb (250 g) asparagus, tough ends removed and spears cut diagonally into ½-inch (12-mm) pieces

2 tsp extra-virgin olive oil

1 medium leek, white and pale green parts only, thinly sliced

Kosher salt and freshly ground pepper

4 eggs

¾ cup (6 fl oz/180 ml) whole milk

¾ cup (6 fl oz/180 ml) heavy cream

½ cup (2 oz/60 g) freshly grated Parmesan cheese

⅛ tsp cayenne pepper

Makes 6–8 servings

Preheat the oven to 375°F (190°C). Prepare the tart or pie shell and pre-bake as directed. Bring a saucepan of generously salted water to a boil. Add the asparagus and cook, uncovered, until tender-crisp, about 3 minutes. Drain the asparagus, then immediately plunge it into a bowl of ice water. When cool, drain again and pat the asparagus dry.

Heat a frying pan over medium heat. Add the olive oil. Stir in the leek with a pinch each of salt and pepper and cook, stirring occasionally, until soft and tender, 4–6 minutes.

In a bowl, whisk together the eggs, milk, cream, Parmesan cheese, cayenne, and a pinch each of salt and pepper. Stir in the asparagus and leek. Pour the mixture into the crust. Bake the quiche until golden on top and just barely jiggling in the center, 45–50 minutes.

Cool the quiche on a rack for at least 20 minutes before slicing. Cut into wedges and serve warm or at room temperature.

broccoli and cheddar quiche

This recipe fuses French technique with the all-American flavors of broccoli and Cheddar cheese. Blanching the broccoli ahead of time keeps the vegetable bright green and tender-crisp, and ensures that it retains a bit of a bite when the quiche is served.

1 prebaked deep tart or pie shell (page 95)

½ lb (250 g) broccoli florets, cut into ½-inch (12-mm) pieces

4 eggs

¾ cup (6 fl oz/180 ml) whole milk

¾ cup (6 fl oz/180 ml) heavy cream

⅛ tsp cayenne pepper

Kosher salt and freshly ground pepper

1 cup (4 oz/125 g) coarsely grated Cheddar cheese

Makes 6–8 servings

Preheat the oven to 375°F (190°C). Prepare the tart or pie shell and prebake as directed. Bring a saucepan of generously salted water to a boil. Add the broccoli and cook until tender-crisp, about 3 minutes. Drain the broccoli, then immediately plunge it into a bowl of ice water. When cool, drain again and pat the broccoli dry.

In a bowl, whisk together the eggs, milk, cream, cayenne, and a pinch each of salt and pepper. Stir in the broccoli and Cheddar cheese. Pour the mixture into the crust. Bake the quiche until golden on top and just barely jiggling in the center, 45–50 minutes.

Cool the quiche on a rack for at least 20 minutes before slicing. Cut into wedges and serve warm or at room temperature.

sausage and mushroom strata

Imagine a savory baked French toast: tender slices of bread soaked in a rich custard, spicy Italian sausages, and smoky Gouda cheese. Perfect for a cozy weekend brunch, this hearty strata is also substantial enough for dinner. Serve with a simple mixed green salad.

6 eggs

2 cups (16 fl oz/500 ml) whole milk

1 cup (8 fl oz/250 ml) heavy cream

2 tbsp freshly grated Parmesan cheese

2 tbsp chopped fresh flat-leaf parsley

Kosher salt and freshly ground pepper

1 tsp canola oil

1 lb (500 g) Italian-style chicken sausages, casings removed

½ lb (250 g) cremini or button mushrooms, or a combination, sliced

1 loaf country-style bread, sliced ½ inch (12 mm) thick

2 cups (8 oz/250 g) grated smoked Gouda cheese

Makes 6 servings

Butter a 13-by-9-inch (33-by-23-cm) glass baking dish. In a bowl, whisk together the eggs, milk, cream, Parmesan cheese, parsley, and a pinch each of salt and pepper.

Heat the oil in a frying pan over medium heat. Add the sausage, using a wooden spoon to break it into bite-size pieces. Cook, stirring occasionally, until the sausage just begins to lose its pink color, 2–3 minutes. Add the mushrooms with a pinch each of salt and pepper and cover the pan, cooking until the mushrooms begin to wilt, about 2 minutes. Remove the cover and continue cooking, stirring occasionally, until the sausage is cooked through and the mushrooms are tender, 3–4 minutes more. Using a slotted spoon, transfer the sausage and mushrooms to paper towels.

Arrange half of the bread on the bottom of the baking dish. Top with half of the egg mixture, half of the Gouda cheese, and half of the sausage and mushroom mixture. Repeat the layering, using all the remaining ingredients. Using a spatula, press on the top layer of bread to be sure it is covered in the custard. Let the strata stand for 30 minutes at room temperature, occasionally pressing on it with the spatula to keep the bread well coated.

Preheat the oven to 350°F (180°C). Bake the strata until golden brown, puffed, and set, about 1 hour. Halfway through the cooking time, remove the strata from the oven and press on the top layer of bread, keeping it submerged in the custard. Let the strata rest for 10 minutes, then serve.

herbed tomato strata

Bright with fresh herbs and tangy ripe tomatoes, this savory strata is wonderful on its own for breakfast. With crisp roasted chicken, it can be transformed into the perfect summer side dish. For a simple yet stylish summer lunch, top each serving with lightly dressed arugula.

6 eggs

2 cups (16 fl oz/500 ml) whole milk

1 cup (8 fl oz/250 ml) heavy cream

2 tbsp freshly grated Parmesan cheese

1 tbsp chopped fresh thyme

2 tsp chopped fresh flat-leaf (Italian) parsley

1 tsp minced fresh sage

Kosher salt and freshly ground pepper

1 loaf country-style bread, cut into ½-inch (12-mm) thick slices

2 cups (8 oz/250 g) grated whole-milk mozzarella cheese

3 medium multicolored tomatoes, diced

Makes 6 servings

Butter a 13-by-9-inch (33-by-23-cm) glass baking dish. In a bowl, whisk together the eggs, milk, cream, Parmesan, thyme, parsley, sage, and a pinch each of salt and pepper.

Arrange half of the sliced bread on the bottom of the baking dish. Top with half of the egg mixture, half of the mozzarella cheese, and half of the chopped tomatoes. Repeat the layering, using all the remaining ingredients. Let the strata stand for 30 minutes at room temperature, occasionally pressing on the ingredients with a spatula to keep the bread well coated.

Preheat the oven to 350°F (180°C). Bake the strata until golden brown, puffed, and set, about 1 hour. Halfway through the cooking time, remove the strata from the oven and press on the top layer of bread, keeping it submerged in the custard. Let the strata rest for about 10 minutes. Cut into squares and serve right away.

savory egg tarts

Sweet butternut squash, earthy sage, and hearty Swiss chard combine with fresh eggs for incredibly flavorful little tarts, which make an unexpected and delightful starter or a light main course for lunch or dinner. The tarts can be assembled in advance—just add the eggs before baking.

8 prebaked individual tart shells (page 95)

1 tbsp extra-virgin olive oil

1 small onion, finely diced

Kosher salt and freshly ground pepper

½ lb (250 g) butternut squash, peeled, seeded, and finely diced

1 tsp minced fresh sage

1 lb (500 g) Swiss chard, stems removed and leaves chopped

Pinch of sugar

1 cup (4 oz/125 g) coarsely grated fontina cheese

8 eggs

Makes 8 servings

Preheat the oven to 375°F (190°C). Prepare the tart shells and prebake as directed. Leave the tart shells on the rimmed baking sheet.

Heat the olive oil in a frying pan over medium heat. Add the onion with a pinch each of salt and pepper and cook, stirring occasionally, until the onion just begins to soften, 2–3 minutes. Add the squash and sage and continue cooking until the onion is soft and translucent and the squash is softened, about 4 minutes more.

Add the chard, sugar, and a pinch each of salt and pepper. Stir well, cover the pan, and cook until the leaves begin to wilt, 2–3 minutes. Remove the cover and stir the chard well, continuing to cook until the leaves are wilted and most of the moisture has evaporated, about 2 minutes more. Transfer the mixture to a bowl and let cool for about 10 minutes. Add the fontina, and stir to combine.

Divide the squash mixture evenly among the tart shells, filling them just below the top. Bake until the cheese is just melted, 4–6 minutes.

Remove the baking sheet from the oven and increase the oven temperature to 425°F (220°C). Crack an egg on top of each tart, sprinkle with a pinch each of salt and pepper, and return to the oven. Bake until the egg whites are just opaque and the yolk is still a bit runny, about 5 minutes. Remove from the oven, unmold the tarts and transfer to plates, and serve.

baked eggs with tarragon and cream

Baked eggs are a restaurant-worthy dish, each guest getting his or her own creamy, rich tarragon-scented serving. The eggs can stand alone as a first course, or they can serve as the centerpiece at brunch accompanied by fresh sliced ham and buttery brioche.

¼ cup (2 fl oz/60 ml) heavy cream

2 tsp chopped fresh tarragon, plus extra leaves for garnish

2 tsp chopped fresh flat-leaf (Italian) parsley

Kosher salt and freshly ground pepper

2 tbsp butter

4 eggs

Makes 4 servings

Preheat the broiler and position the rack about 4 inches (10 cm) from the heat source. Place four ½-cup (125-ml) heatproof ramekins on a rimmed baking sheet. In a small bowl, whisk together the cream, 2 teaspoons tarragon, parsley, and a pinch each of salt and pepper.

Place 1½ teaspoons of the cream mixture and ½ tablespoon of the butter in each ramekin. Place ramekins under the broiler until the mixture is hot and bubbling around the edges, 1–2 minutes. Immediately crack an egg into each dish, top each with another 1½ teaspoons of the cream mixture, and sprinkle with a pinch each of salt and pepper. Return the baking sheet to the oven and cook until the egg whites are opaque and the yolks are still a bit runny, 4–5 minutes more.

Place each ramekin on a plate and top with a couple of tarragon leaves. Serve right away.

eggs baked in tomatoes

Here's a new twist on baked eggs—a whole egg baked inside of a hollowed-out tomato, topped with nutty Parmesan cheese and ribbons of sweet basil. Ripe but firm tomatoes are a must here—they are sturdy enough to hold up to the oven but lend lots of sweet juices to infuse the eggs.

4 medium tomatoes

Kosher salt and freshly ground pepper

4 eggs

1/4 cup (1 oz/30 g) freshly grated Parmesan cheese

1 tbsp extra-virgin olive oil

1/4 cup (1/4 oz/7 g) fresh basil, cut into thin ribbons

Makes 4 servings

Preheat the oven to 450°F (230°C). Line a rimmed baking sheet with aluminum foil. Cut off the top quarter of each tomato. Carefully scoop out the insides of the tomatoes, leaving a cup about 1/2-inch (12-mm) thick. Reserve the insides for another use or discard. Place the hollowed-out tomatoes on the prepared baking sheet and sprinkle the insides with a pinch each of salt and pepper.

Crack an egg into each tomato and sprinkle 1 tablespoon of the Parmesan over each egg. Place the baking sheet in the oven and bake until the egg whites are opaque and the yolks are still a bit runny, 8–10 minutes.

Remove the egg-stuffed tomatoes from the oven. Drizzle the tops with olive oil and scatter evenly with the basil. Place each tomato on a plate and serve right away.

eggs baked in prosciutto nests

Thin slices of prosciutto baked in individual ramekins crisp up to form delicate cups for creamy baked eggs. Lined with buttery brioche toast and dotted with lemon zest and chives, this is an inspiring and fun way to serve your eggs that tastes as good as it looks.

12 very thin slices
prosciutto di Parma

6 small slices brioche
bread, each ½-inch
(12-mm) thick

1 tbsp butter,
at room temperature

Kosher salt and
freshly ground pepper

6 eggs

Finely grated zest of
1 small lemon

1 tbsp minced
fresh chives

Makes 6 servings

Preheat the oven to 400°F (200°C). Lightly oil six ½-cup (4–fl oz/125-ml) ramekins or custard cups and place on a rimmed baking sheet.

Line each ramekin with 2 slices of prosciutto, letting the prosciutto hang over a bit, pressing it gently into the bottom. Using a round cutter about the diameter of the ramekin bottoms, cut 6 rounds out of the brioche. Butter each side of the bread rounds and place a bread round into each prosciutto-lined ramekin. Bake until the bread is golden brown, about 5 minutes, then remove the baking sheet from the oven and increase the heat to 450°F (230°C).

Crack 1 egg into each ramekin. Sprinkle evenly with lemon zest, chives, and a pinch each of salt and pepper. Continue baking until the egg whites are opaque and the yolks are still a bit runny, 8–10 minutes more. Let rest for about 2 minutes. Serve right away.

other egg dishes

international inspiration

Fried, boiled, scrambled, and poached, this chapter has a little of everything, including flavors from around the world. The recipes trot the globe, from Mexican-influenced breakfast burritos to a French croque madame to all-American deviled eggs and egg salad sandwiches.

setting up for success

From spicy south-of-the-border chilaquiles and hearty huevos rancheros to classically French eggs Benedict and fresh California-influenced variations, this chapter covers a host of other egg favorites. For tips on scrambling or frying eggs, see pages 102 or 103.

boiling eggs

Hard-boiled or soft-boiled might seem like the easiest way to prepare eggs, but following a few simple rules will ensure they are flawless. Always put the eggs in cold water to start, bring the water to a boil, then cover the pan and shut off the heat. This ensures that the eggs cook slowly and don't crack against the sides of the pan. When they are cooked too long at an overly high temperature, the outside of the yolks can develop an unappealing green cast.

SOFT-BOILED These eggs are cooked in their shell until the whites are opaque and the yolks are hot and runny. Soft-boiled eggs are traditionally eaten directly from the shell in an eggcup, often with strips of toast.

HARD-BOILED Always popular, hard-boiled eggs are delicious on their own and can be made into deviled eggs or egg salad. They are also great chopped and added to salads or sprinkled over grilled asparagus.

poaching eggs

Poached eggs are cooked in simmering water until the whites are set and opaque, and the yolk is runny. They are most commonly served in eggs Benedict or perched atop corned beef hash. While they might seem intimidating to prepare, by following a few tips you can make perfect poached eggs every time (for step-by-step instructions see pages 88 and 105).

USE FRESH EGGS Always try to use the freshest grade AA eggs you can find. They will hold their shape better and you'll get the best results.

CHOOSE THE RIGHT PAN Choose a deep, wide sauté pan so that the eggs have a lot of space between one another while they are poaching.

ADD AN ACIDIC INGREDIENT TO THE WATER Adding white vinegar or lemon juice to the water will help the egg whites set more quickly.

CRACK EACH EGG INTO A BOWL Crack the eggs into a small cup or ramekin. Lower the cup until it just touches the water, then tilt it slightly and let the egg slip into the water. Repeat to add more eggs. Only cook as many eggs at one time as will comfortably fit in the pan.

KEEP EGGS WARM If you are making a lot of eggs, or just want to keep them warm while putting together the rest of the meal, you can hold them for up to 10 minutes in a bowl of hot (not boiling) water. Just remove the eggs with a slotted spoon when they are done and gently place them into the bowl of water.

FINISH THE EGGS For perfect edges on your poached eggs, hold the egg in a slotted spoon, and trim any ragged edges with kitchen shears.

eggs from around the world

Nearly every culture uses eggs in some way, from Italian frittatas and French omelets and quiches to hearty Mexican breakfasts with eggs, salsa and beans. Eggs are panfried with rice, meat and vegetables for Chinese fried rice, and are also an essential part of the savory Indian rice dish biryani. Here are a few other ideas:

Top creamy polenta with a poached egg and Parmesan.

For a Southern treat, slip a fried egg inside a biscuit with country-style ham.

Crack an egg on top of your homemade pizza right after you slide it into the oven.

croque madame

*This French rendition of the American ham and cheese sandwich is comfort food at its
very best, and worth every decadent bite. Creamy béchamel sauce, nutty Gruyère cheese,
and smoky ham nestle inside pan-toasted bread, with a fried egg crowning the top.*

1 cup (8 fl oz/250 ml)
Béchamel Sauce
(page 96)

8 slices good-quality
white sandwich bread

3 tbsp butter,
at room temperature

1 tbsp Dijon mustard

¼ lb (125 g)
Gruyère cheese, grated

8 thin slices
smoked country ham

4 eggs

Kosher salt and
freshly ground pepper

2 tbsp chopped fresh
flat-leaf (Italian) parsley

Makes 4 servings

Prepare the béchamel sauce and keep warm. Lay the bread slices on a work surface and, using 2 tablespoons of the butter in total, butter one side of each slice. Turn 4 slices over and brush them with the mustard.

Heat a large nonstick frying pan or griddle over medium heat. Add 4 slices of the buttered bread, without the Dijon, buttered side down in a single layer. Spread each bread slice with a spoonful of the sauce, add enough cheese to cover the sauce, and top each with 2 slices of ham. Put one of the remaining bread slices, buttered side up, on each sandwich. Cook until the Gruyère begins to melt and the bread is nicely browned on both sides, turning once, 3–4 minutes. Press gently on the sandwiches with a spatula to help melt the cheese.

Meanwhile, melt the remaining 1 tablespoon of butter in another large nonstick frying pan over medium heat. Crack the eggs into the pan and sprinkle them with salt and pepper. Let the eggs cook until the white begins to turn opaque, 2–3 minutes. If desired, turn the eggs over and cook until the yolk just begins to set, about 30 seconds more.

To serve, place each sandwich on a plate. Top each sandwich with another spoonful of béchamel sauce and a fried egg. Sprinkle with the parsley and serve right away.

chilaquiles

Traditionally eaten to cure what ails you in the morning, this Mexican breakfast dish is savory enough for any time of day. Tender chicken and crisp tortillas are simmered in a spicy sauce then topped with a fried egg, but they are equally delicious with scrambled eggs.

2 tsp canola oil

1 medium white onion, thinly sliced

Kosher salt and freshly ground pepper

2 tsp minced garlic

1 can (28 oz/875 g) diced tomatoes in juice

2 chipotle chiles in adobo sauce, chopped

2 cups (16 fl oz/500 ml) chicken stock

2 cups (¾ lb/370 g) shredded cooked chicken

8 oz (250 g) tortilla chips

2 tbsp butter

4 eggs

½ cup (2 oz/60 g) grated Cotija cheese

2 radishes, thinly sliced

1 tbsp chopped fresh cilantro

Makes 4 servings

Warm 1 teaspoon of the canola oil in a saucepan over medium heat. Add the onion with a pinch each of salt and pepper. Cook, stirring occasionally, until the onion is tender, 4–6 minutes. Add the garlic and cook, stirring, until fragrant, 1 minute more. Add the tomatoes and chipotle chiles and stir to combine. Bring the mixture to a boil, then reduce the heat to medium. Cook until the onion is soft, 4–5 minutes more. Carefully transfer the mixture to a blender and purée until smooth.

Warm the remaining 1 teaspoon of canola oil in the saucepan over medium heat and, when hot, add the tomato mixture. Stir in the chicken stock, then season to taste with salt and pepper. Cook the sauce until it is slightly reduced and thickened, 8–10 minutes. Stir in the shredded chicken and cook just to warm through, 2–3 minutes. Stir in the tortilla chips and remove the pan from the heat.

Melt the butter in a large nonstick frying pan over medium heat. Crack the eggs into the pan and sprinkle them with salt and pepper. Let the eggs cook until the white begins to turn opaque, 2–3 minutes. Turn the eggs over and continue cooking until the yolks are just barely set, about 30 seconds more.

Divide the *chilaquiles* between four plates. Top each with a fried egg and sprinkle with the Cotija, radishes, and cilantro. Serve right away.

breakfast burrito

The ideal on-the-go breakfast, warm flour tortillas are wrapped around a cheesy chorizo scramble with creamy avocado slices and fresh homemade salsa. Feel free to experiment by adding your own favorite ingredients, such as black beans or cooked shredded chicken.

Fresh Tomato Salsa (page 97)

8 eggs

2 tbsp milk

2 tbsp chopped fresh cilantro

Kosher salt and freshly ground pepper

Cayenne pepper

1 tsp canola oil

½ white onion, diced

½ lb (250 g) Mexican-style chorizo (uncooked), casings removed

4 large flour tortillas

½ cup (2 oz/60 g) Monterey jack cheese

1 avocado, pitted, peeled, and sliced

Makes 4 servings

Prepare the tomato salsa as directed and set aside. In a bowl, whisk together the eggs, milk, cilantro, a pinch each of salt and pepper, and a pinch of cayenne. Continue whisking until the eggs are nice and frothy.

Warm the oil in a nonstick frying pan over medium heat. Add the onion with a pinch each of salt, pepper, and cayenne and cook, stirring occasionally, until the onion just begins to soften, 3–4 minutes. Stir in the chorizo, breaking it into small pieces with a wooden spoon. Cook, stirring, until the chorizo is cooked through and the onion is soft and translucent.

Reduce the heat to medium-low and add the eggs. Let the mixture cook until the eggs just begin to set, about 1 minute. Using a heatproof rubber spatula, gently stir the eggs around the pan, letting any uncooked egg run onto the bottom of the pan. Stir gently, cooking until the eggs have set, about 2–3 minutes more.

Warm the tortillas in a low oven, a frying pan, or the microwave. Place each tortilla on a plate and sprinkle each with 2 tablespoons of the cheese. Place one-quarter of the egg mixture in the center of each tortilla, along with a heaping spoonful of salsa and a few avocado slices. Roll the tortilla over the filling, folding in the sides to encase it, and continue rolling to form the burrito. Serve right away.

huevos rancheros

The hearty and healthful south-of-the-border ingredients in this dish—tomato, onion, black beans, queso fresco, avocado, tortillas, and of course eggs—offer something for everyone. If you are short on time, use your favorite store-bought salsa instead of making your own.

Fresh Tomato Salsa (page 97)

1 can (14 oz/440 g) black beans, drained and rinsed

1 chipotle chile, seeded and chopped, plus 1 tsp of the adobo sauce

1 tbsp canola oil

4 good-quality corn tortillas

2 tbsp butter

4 eggs

Kosher salt and freshly ground pepper

1 avocado, pitted, peeled, and sliced

¼ cup (1¼ oz/40 g) crumbled *queso fresco*

Makes 4 servings

Prepare the tomato salsa as directed and set aside. In a small saucepan, combine the black beans with the chipotle chile and adobo sauce. Stir well, crushing the beans slightly, and heat over medium heat until warmed through.

Warm the canola oil in a large nonstick frying pan over medium heat. Add the tortillas, 1–2 at a time, just to warm through, about 30 seconds for each side. Place each tortilla on a plate.

Wipe out any excess oil from the pan and reduce the heat to medium-low. Melt the butter in the pan, then add the eggs and sprinkle them with a pinch each of salt and pepper. Let the eggs cook until the white begins to turn opaque, 2–3 minutes. Turn the eggs over and continue cooking until the yolks just begin to set, about 30 seconds more.

Spoon one-quarter of the beans over the tortillas on each plate, spreading them to cover most of the tortilla. Top each plate with an egg, a large spoonful of the salsa, a few avocado slices, and sprinkle with some of the *queso fresco*. Serve right away.

easy eggs benedict

A light and creamy hollandaise plus perfectly poached eggs are essential to the very best eggs Benedict. This is definitely breakfast for a special morning. Canadian bacon is the classic ingredient in this dish, but you can substitute thin slices of ham if you'd like.

1 cup (8 fl oz/250 ml)
Hollandaise Sauce
(page 96)

4 English muffins,
halved

2 tsp white or
cider vinegar

Kosher salt

8 eggs

8 slices Canadian bacon

1–2 tbsp butter,
at room temperature

2 tbsp chopped fresh
flat-leaf (Italian) parsley

Makes 4 servings

Prepare the hollandaise sauce and set aside to keep warm. Preheat the broiler and place the muffin halves on a rimmed baking sheet.

Fill a wide, straight-sided pan, such as a sauté pan, three-quarters full of water. Stir in the vinegar and a pinch of salt. Bring the water to a boil, then reduce the heat to medium-low so the water is just simmering. Fill a bowl halfway with hot tap water and set it next to the stove.

One at a time, crack the eggs into a ramekin or small cup and gently pour it into the water. Cook as many eggs at a time as will comfortably fit in the pan. Let each egg cook until the white begins to set, about 2 minutes, then gently turn the egg over with a slotted spoon. Let cook for another minute or so, until the white is opaque and fully cooked and the yolk is still runny. Carefully transfer the eggs with the slotted spoon to the bowl of water to keep warm while you finish cooking the rest of the eggs.

Warm a frying pan over medium heat, and add the Canadian bacon. Cook until warmed through, turning once, about 2 minutes total. Toast the muffin halves under the broiler until golden brown. Lightly butter the toasted muffins and place two halves on each plate. Top each muffin half with a slice of Canadian bacon, a warm egg, and about 2 tablespoons of the warm hollandaise sauce. Sprinkle with parsley and serve right away.

eggs benedict variations

Variations on eggs Benedict are limited only by your imagination. Experiment with ingredients such as sliced tomatoes and crisp bacon, fresh lump crabmeat, or smoked salmon. Use the combinations below as a starting point to personalize your own version of this breakfast classic.

BLACKSTONE — Instead of Canadian bacon, cook 8 slices smoked bacon until crisp. Cut each slice of bacon in half and place 2 pieces on each muffin half, then top with a slice of fresh ripe tomato, an egg, and hollandaise.

FLORENTINE — Instead of Canadian bacon, place about ¼ cup (¼ oz/7 g) firmly packed baby spinach leaves on each muffin half before adding the eggs and the sauce. Sprinkle with chopped fresh marjoram, about 2 teaspoons total, instead of parsley.

SMOKED SALMON — Instead of Canadian bacon, place a large slice of smoked salmon on each muffin half before adding the eggs and the sauce. Sprinkle with chopped fresh dill, about 2 teaspoons total, instead of parsley.

CRAB — Instead of Canadian bacon, place about ¼ cup (4 oz/125 g) fresh crabmeat with a pinch each of salt and pepper on each muffin half before adding the eggs and the sauce. Sprinkle with chopped fresh chives, about 2 teaspoons total, instead of parsley.

HAM AND AVOCADO — Instead of Canadian bacon, place thin slices of smoked ham on each muffin half, then top the ham with a few slices of avocado before adding the eggs and the sauce.

deviled eggs

The perfect two-bite snack, deviled eggs have been popular party food for generations. This updated version includes fresh thyme, minced shallots, and tart cornichons, which adds a little crunch. The sprinkle of cayenne pepper adds just enough "devil" to the filling.

8 eggs

¼ cup (2 fl oz/60 ml) mayonnaise

1 tbsp whole-grain mustard

1 tbsp minced shallots

5 cornichons, minced

½ tsp cayenne pepper

1½ tsp minced fresh thyme

Kosher salt and freshly ground pepper

Makes 4 servings

Place the eggs in a saucepan with enough cold water to cover them by 1 inch (2.5 cm). Bring to a boil over medium-high heat. Remove the pan from the heat, cover, and let stand for 14 minutes. Drain the eggs, then transfer them to a bowl of ice water to cool for at least 5 minutes.

Peel the eggs and cut them in half lengthwise. Carefully scoop the yolks into a bowl. Place the whites, cut side up, on a serving plate.

Use a fork to mash the yolks until smooth. Add the mayonnaise, mustard, shallots, cornichons, cayenne, 1 teaspoon of the thyme, and a pinch each of salt and pepper. Whip the mixture together until light and fluffy.

Using a small spoon, scoop the yolk mixture into the egg white halves. Alternatively, transfer the yolk mixture to a small plastic bag, cut a ½-inch (12-mm) hole in one corner, and pipe the mixture into the whites. Top the eggs with a sprinkle of the remaining thyme.

egg salad sandwiches

A creamy egg salad sandwich can transport you straight back to childhood. This version updates the classic for adulthood, with sweet Spanish piquillo peppers, fresh cilantro, and toasty cumin. If you can't find piquillo peppers, feel free to substitute a roasted red bell pepper.

8 eggs

½ cup (4 fl oz/125 ml) mayonnaise

1 tbsp Dijon mustard

2 jarred roasted *piquillo* peppers, diced

2 tbsp minced celery

1 tbsp chopped fresh cilantro

¼ tsp ground cumin

Kosher salt and freshly ground pepper

8 slices crusty country bread

4 large lettuce leaves

Makes 4 servings

Place the eggs in a saucepan with enough cold water to cover them by 1 inch (2.5 cm). Bring to a boil over medium-high heat. Remove the pan from the heat, cover, and let stand for 14 minutes. Drain the eggs, then transfer them to a bowl of ice water to cool for at least 5 minutes.

Peel the eggs and coarsely chop them. Transfer the eggs to a bowl and stir in ⅓ cup (2½ fl oz/80 ml) of the mayonnaise, the mustard, *piquillo* peppers, celery, cilantro, cumin, and a pinch each of salt and pepper. Mix well to combine, then season to taste with additional salt and pepper if needed. The egg salad can be covered and refrigerated for up to 2 days.

When ready to make sandwiches, lay the bread slices on a work surface. Spread each slice with a very thin layer of the remaining mayonnaise. Divide the egg salad between 4 of the bread slices, then top with the lettuce leaves. Cover each with a bread slice and serve right away.

basic recipes

From flaky pastry dough for your quiches and tarts to simple sauces and vegetable prep, this section of the book will enable you to prepare all the recipes in this book from scratch. If time is an issue, you can purchase most of these items in well-stocked delis or markets.

savory pastry dough

1¾ cups (9 oz/280 g) all-purpose flour
Kosher salt
9 tbsp (4½ oz/135 g) cold butter, cut into small pieces
1 egg yolk
2 tbsp heavy cream
3 tbsp ice-cold water

Makes one 10-by-2-inch (25-by-5-cm) deep tart shell, or one 11-inch (28-cm) pie shell, or eight 4½-inch (11.5-cm) individual tart shells

Place the flour and a generous pinch of salt in a food processor and pulse just to combine. Add the butter and pulse until the mixture resembles coarse meal, about 10 times. In a small bowl, whisk together the egg yolk and cream, add it to the food processor, and pulse a couple of times to combine. Add the water, 1 tablespoon at a time, until the dough holds together when squeezed in your hand. Turn the dough out onto a work surface and gently knead it into a ball. Press the dough into a disk and wrap with plastic wrap.

Refrigerate for 30 minutes or up to overnight. When ready to use, remove the plastic wrap. On a floured work surface, roll the dough out into a circle, about 12 inches (30 cm) in diameter.

To make a deep tart or pie shell, remove the top sheet of plastic and gently invert the dough into a 10-by-2-inch (25-by-5-cm) quiche pan or an 11-inch (28-cm) pie pan, folding over any overhanging dough to create a rim. Crimp if desired. Place the dough in the freezer until firm, at least 20 minutes or up to overnight.

To prebake the tart or pie shell, preheat the oven to 375°F (190°C). Line the shell with parchment paper or aluminum foil and fill it with pie weights or dried beans. Bake the crust until dry and set, 15–17 minutes. Carefully remove the parchment and pie weights and continue baking the crust until golden brown, about 10 minutes more. Remove from the oven and let cool on a rack.

To make individual tart shells, line a baking sheet with parchment paper. Cut the dough into eight

6-inch (15-cm) circles. Set eight 4½-inch (11.5-cm) tart pans or flan rings on the prepared baking sheet and place a round of dough in each one, gently pressing it into the sides. Place the baking sheet in the freezer until the dough is very firm, about 20 minutes.

To prebake the tart shells, preheat the oven to 375°F (190°C). Line each tart shell with a round of parchment paper and fill it with pie weights or beans. Bake until the crusts are dry and set, 8–10 minutes. Carefully remove the parchment and pie weights and continue baking the tart shells until golden brown and fully cooked, 6–8 minutes more. Remove from the oven and let cool on a rack until ready to use.

hollandaise sauce

3 egg yolks
1 tbsp freshly squeezed lemon juice
Kosher salt and freshly ground pepper
Cayenne pepper
½ cup (4 oz/125 g) butter, melted and hot

Makes about 1 cup (8 fl oz/250 ml)

Place the egg yolks in a blender with the lemon juice and a pinch each of salt, pepper, and cayenne. Blend on low speed for a few seconds, just until liquid. With the motor on low, very slowly add the ½ cup melted butter, blending until the sauce is nice and thick. If the sauce is too thick at this point, add a bit of very hot water.

Taste and season as needed with salt, pepper, and lemon juice. Transfer the sauce to a thermos or a double boiler over very low heat to keep warm.

béchamel sauce

2 tsp butter, at room temperature
2 tbsp all-purpose flour
2 tsp dry mustard
1 cup (8 fl oz/250 ml) milk
Kosher salt and freshly ground pepper
Pinch of cayenne pepper

Makes about 1 cup (8 fl oz/250 ml)

In a saucepan, melt the butter over medium heat. Add the flour and dry mustard and whisk until well incorporated, about 1 minute. Reduce the heat to medium-low, add the milk, and whisk constantly until the mixture comes to a boil and thickens, 2–3 minutes more. Season the sauce to taste with salt, pepper, and cayenne, cover the pan, and remove it from the heat.

fresh tomato salsa

1 large tomato, diced
½ white onion, diced
1 serrano chile, seeded and minced (optional)
Juice of ½ lime
¼ tsp ground cumin
¼ cup (⅓ oz/10 g) chopped cilantro
Kosher salt and freshly ground pepper

Makes about 1 cup (8 fl oz/250 ml)

In a bowl, combine the tomato, onion, serrano chile (if using), lime juice, cumin, cilantro, and a pinch each of salt and pepper. Stir well and let the salsa stand at room temperature for at least 20 minutes. Taste again and season as needed with more salt and pepper.

roasting chiles or peppers

Poblano chiles or bell peppers

Preheat the broiler and place a rack about 4 inches (10 cm) from the heat source. Line a rimmed baking sheet with aluminum foil.

Cut the chiles or peppers in half lengthwise and remove the ribs, seeds, and stem. Place the chiles or peppers, cut side down, on the baking sheet. Roast the chiles or peppers, turning as needed,

until blackened all over but not charred. Transfer to a heatproof bowl, cover with plastic wrap, and let steam for 5 minutes. Using wet fingers, peel the blackened skin from the chiles or peppers.

roasting garlic

Garlic cloves, unpeeled

Preheat the broiler and place a rack about 4 inches (10 cm) from the heat source. Line a rimmed baking sheet with aluminum foil. Add the garlic cloves to the baking sheet, leaving the skins intact. Roast until blackened all over but not charred. Transfer to a heatproof bowl, cover with plastic wrap, and let steam for 5 minutes. Using wet fingers, pop the garlic cloves from their skins.

Note: Garlic can be roasted alongside the chiles if used in the same recipe

preparing artichoke bottoms

2 medium artichokes

Fill a bowl with cold water and lemon juice. Remove the leaves of the artichoke by pulling them back until they break. Slice the inner leaves off and, using a spoon, scoop out the hairy choke and leaves. Trim the base, and then place in the lemon-water until ready to use.

fillings for scrambles, omelets, frittatas, and quiche

One of the best things about eggs is their versatility, and few dishes are more welcoming to an array of ingredient combinations than scrambles, omelets, frittatas, and quiches. Here you will find many ideas for ingredients as well as suggestions for delicious combinations.

Cheeses

Shredded firm cheese such as sharp Cheddar or Gruyère; grated aged cheese such as Parmesan or *pecorino;* crumbled blue cheese, such as Gorgonzola; crumbled fresh goat cheese; sliced soft cheeses such as Brie; cubed cream cheese; cubed or sliced fresh mozzarella cheese; dollops of fresh ricotta cheese

Fresh herbs

Fresh flat-leaf (Italian) parsley, rosemary, basil, tarragon, chives, thyme, oregano, marjoram

Vegetables

Diced tomatoes, halved cherry tomatoes, sautéed mushrooms, caramelized onions, blanched asparagus or broccoli, sautéed leeks, roasted chiles, roasted bell peppers, sautéed spinach or chard, arugula, green onions, corn kernels

Meats

Cooked sliced sausage, diced ham, cooked crumbled bacon, cooked diced pancetta, thinly sliced prosciutto, cooked shredded chicken

Seafood

Lump crabmeat; cooked bay shrimp; cooked, peeled, and deveined shrimp; smoked salmon; smoked whitefish

A finishing touch

Fresh tomato salsa, roasted tomatillo salsa, marinara sauce, chopped cherry tomatoes, minced fresh herbs, sour cream or crème fraîche

Yummy combinations

○ Sautéed mushrooms, thyme, and fontina cheese

○ Blanched asparagus and fresh goat cheese

○ Sautéed spinach, crumbled bacon, and Cheddar

○ Roasted corn kernels, green onions, crumbled bacon, and Monterey jack cheese

○ Roasted bell peppers, sautéed onions, Italian sausage, fresh oregano, and marinara sauce

○ Sliced prosciutto, fresh mozzarella, and arugula

○ Cooked bay shrimp, sautéed leeks and asparagus, and fresh tarragon

○ Caramelized onions, rosemary, and blue cheese

○ Roasted chiles, Mexican chorizo, and Cheddar

menu ideas

Here are a whole host of menu suggestions for serving egg dishes, whether it's for a simple family breakfast, a hearty weekend brunch, a light summertime lunch, or a special holiday buffet. Each includes a recipe from the book, plus side dish recommendations and drinks.

summertime brunch

cherry tomato, mozzarella, and basil frittata (page 40), grilled chicken-apple sausages, peach bellini

∞∞∞

hearty weekend brunch

steak and eggs (page 18), hash browned potatoes, buttered sourdough toast with jam, coffee or tea

∞∞∞

winter lunch

savory egg tarts (page 73), frisee salad with pancetta and citrus vinaigrette, bloody marys

∞∞∞

holiday brunch buffet

roasted red pepper and potato frittata (page 52), sausage and mushroom strata (page 69), buttery biscuits with honey, sliced glazed ham, mixed citrus salad, mimosas

all-american breakfast

ham and cheddar omelet (page 30), pan-fried potatoes and onions, buttered whole-wheat toast, orange juice

∞∞∞

mexican brunch

chilaquiles (page 84), spicy refried beans, warm corn tortillas, horchata or aqua fresca

∞∞∞

spanish lunch

fried eggs with sweet pepper pipérade (page 14), thinly sliced jamón serrano, roasted potato wedges with paprika, cava or light sparkling wine

∞∞∞

light french supper

asparagus and leek quiche (page 67), mâche or mixed greens salad with fresh goats cheese, dry white wine

scrambling eggs

1. Beat the eggs
Break the eggs into a bowl and add a pinch each of salt and pepper. Some recipes may call for water, milk, or cream to be added. Beat the eggs with a whisk or fork until frothy.

2. Pour the eggs into the pan
Place a nonstick frying pan over medium heat and add a small amount of butter or oil. When the butter is melted, pour in the beaten eggs and reduce the heat to medium-low.

3. Cook the eggs
Cook the eggs until they just begin to set, about 1 minute. Using a heatproof rubber spatula, push the firmer eggs toward the center of the pan, letting any uncooked eggs run on to the bottom of the pan. The more you stir, the smaller the curds will be.

4. Check the consistency
If you like soft, moist eggs, cook them for about 4 minutes. For firmer, drier eggs, cook them for 7–8 minutes. Serve right away.

frying eggs

1. Melt the butter

Place a nonstick frying pan over medium heat and add butter or oil. If desired, crack an egg into a small bowl.

2. Add the eggs to the pan

When the butter is melted, carefully slide the egg into the pan. Reduce the heat to low and cook until the whites begin to turn opaque and the yolks thicken, 2–3 minutes.

3. For eggs sunny-side up:

Tilt the pan and spoon the pooled butter or oil from the edge. Drizzle the butter or oil over the eggs to baste them. Slide the eggs onto a plate and serve right away.

4. For eggs over easy, over medium, or over hard:

Use a nonstick spatula to flip the eggs over gently. Cook for about 30 seconds for eggs over easy, about 1 minute for eggs over medium, and about 1½ minutes for eggs over hard. Serve right away.

boiling eggs

1. Boil the eggs

Place the eggs in a saucepan with enough cold water to cover them by 1 inch (2.5 cm). Bring to a boil over medium-high heat. Cover the pot and turn off the heat. Let the eggs stand for about 5 minutes for soft-boiled, runny yolks; about 9 minutes for medium-firm yolks; and 14 minutes for hard-boiled eggs.

2. Peel the eggs, if desired

Soft-boiled eggs are often served in their shells. For medium- or hard-boiled eggs, transfer the eggs to an ice bath for at least 5 minutes. Crack the shells gently on the kitchen counter, then peel away and discard.

3. Slice the eggs

To serve, slice medium- or hard-cooked eggs in half or quarters lengthwise, or crosswise into slices, depending upon your recipe.

4. Overcooked eggs

Be sure to watch the timer. Overcooked eggs will have a gray-green ring around the yolks and rubbery whites.

poaching eggs

1. Acidulate the water

Bring a generous amount of water to a boil in a large sauté pan. Add 2 teaspoons of white or cider vinegar or lemon juice. You can also add a pinch of salt. This will help the egg whites form a nicely rounded shape.

2. Crack the egg into a dish

Crack one egg into a ramekin or another small dish. This will help you pour the egg neatly into the hot liquid. Check for shells.

3. Pour the egg into the water

Reduce the heat to medium-low and gently ease the egg into the simmering water. Repeat with the remaining eggs. Gently cook the eggs, using a slotted spoon to turn them over, for 3 minutes if you like runny yolks or 5 minutes if you prefer the yolks more set.

4. Remove the eggs from the water

Using the slotted spoon, gently scoop out the eggs, blot on a paper towel, and serve.

mincing fresh herbs

1. Pluck the leaves

Rinse the herbs and pat dry. Grasp the leaves between your thumb and index finger and pluck them from the stems. Discard the stems and any discolored leaves.

2. Chop the leaves

Gather the leaves on a cutting board. Rest the fingertips of one hand on the tip of a chef's knife and rock the blade back and forth briefly over the leaves to chop coarsely.

3. Finely chop or mince the leaves

Gather the leaves together and rock the blade over them until they are chopped into small, even pieces (finely chopped), or into pieces as fine as possible (minced).

working with chiles

1. Quarter the chile lengthwise
Many cooks wear a disposable latex glove on the hand that touches the chile to prevent irritation from its potent oils. Using a paring knife, cut the chile into halves lengthwise, then into quarters.

2. Remove the seeds and ribs
Using the paring knife, cut away the seeds and ribs from each chile quarter. Capsaicin, the compound that makes chiles hot, is concentrated in these areas; removing them lessens the heat.

3. Slice the quarters into strips
Place the quarters, cut side up, on the cutting board. Cut carefully into narrow strips about ⅛-inch (3-mm) wide.

4. Dice and mince the strips
Line up the chile strips and cut them crosswise at ⅛-inch intervals. Rest the fingertips of one hand on the top of the knife and rock the blade back and forth over the pieces to mince them.

index

weldon**owen**

415 Jackson Street, Suite 200, San Francisco, CA 94111

Telephone: 415 291 0100 Fax: 415 291 8841

www.weldonowen.com

Weldon Owen is a division of

BONNIER

WELDON OWEN INC.

CEO and President Terry Newell

VP, Sales and Marketing Amy Kaneko

Director of Finance Mark Perrigo

VP and Publisher Hannah Rahill

Executive Editor Kim Laidlaw

Creative Director Emma Boys

Art Director Alexandra Zeigler

Senior Designer Ashley Lima

Junior Designer Anna Grace

Production Director Chris Hemesath

Production Manager Michelle Duggan

Color Manager Teri Bell

Photographer   Kate Sears

Food Stylist   Robyn Valarik

Prop Stylist   Natalie Hoelen

EGGS

Conceived and produced by Weldon Owen Inc.

Copyright © 2010 Weldon Owen Inc.

Color separations by Embassy Graphics

Printed and bound in China by 1010 Printing, Ltd.

First printed in 2010

10 9 8 7 6 5

Library of Congress Control Number: 2010938154

ISBN-13: 978-1-61628-066-6

ISBN-10: 1-61628-066-2

ACKNOWLEDGMENTS

Weldon Owen wishes to thank the following people for their generous support in producing this book:
Leslie Evans, Elizabeth Parson, Laurie Pfeiffer, Jane Tunks, and Jason Wheeler

NOTE ABOUT THE RECIPES

Consuming partially cooked eggs can lead to food poisoning from salmonella or other bacteria, though incidence of such contamination is rare. This risk is of most concern to young children, elderly people, pregnant women, and anyone with a compromised immune system. If you have health and safety concerns, you may wish to avoid foods made with undercooked eggs.